TRANSPORTATION IN MY COMMUNITY

AIRPLANES

by Cari Meister

PEBBLE
a capstone imprint

Climb aboard.
Buckle your seatbelt.

Let's fly.

WHOOSH!

Airplanes are amazing flying machines.
They take us all over the world.

How do they work?

A pilot sits in the cockpit.
The instrument panel is inside.

The buttons and switches
help the pilot fly the plane.

BRUMMMMM!

The pilot turns on the plane's
engines. The plane roars to life.
It taxis down the runway.

The plane zooms forward.
It moves faster and faster.

Air flows over its wings.
The plane lifts into the air.

fin

Fins are in the back of the airplane.

fin

The fins help keep the plane level as it flies through the air.

It's time to land.

The plane slows down and descends.
The pilot lowers the landing gear.
Wheels touch down on the runway.

We're here!

It has taken many years to develop the modern airplane.

The first powered airplane was light and airy.
On its first flight, it flew for 59 seconds.

Today we use planes for all kinds of things.
A passenger jet carries people.

It is like a big school bus in the sky.
Some can carry more than 850 people.

A fighter jet is **FAST!**

The fighter pilot sits in this small military plane.
Some fighter jets have missiles and other weapons.
They can shoot down other jets in the sky.

A cargo plane carries goods instead of people.
Super transporters move really big things.

The *Antonov AN-225* is the world's largest cargo plane.
It can hold and move the weight of 80 cars!

WHIRRR!

A crop duster has a propeller.
It helps lift the plane into the air.

Crop dusters spread fertilizer on farm fields.
The fertilizer helps the plants grow.

floats

SPLASH!

A seaplane does not need a runway.
It can take off and land on water.
The plane has floats instead of wheels.

Seaplanes can be used to search
for and rescue people in water.

People are working to make
airplanes faster and safer.
They think up new ideas
and make new designs.

What will they think of next?

Timeline

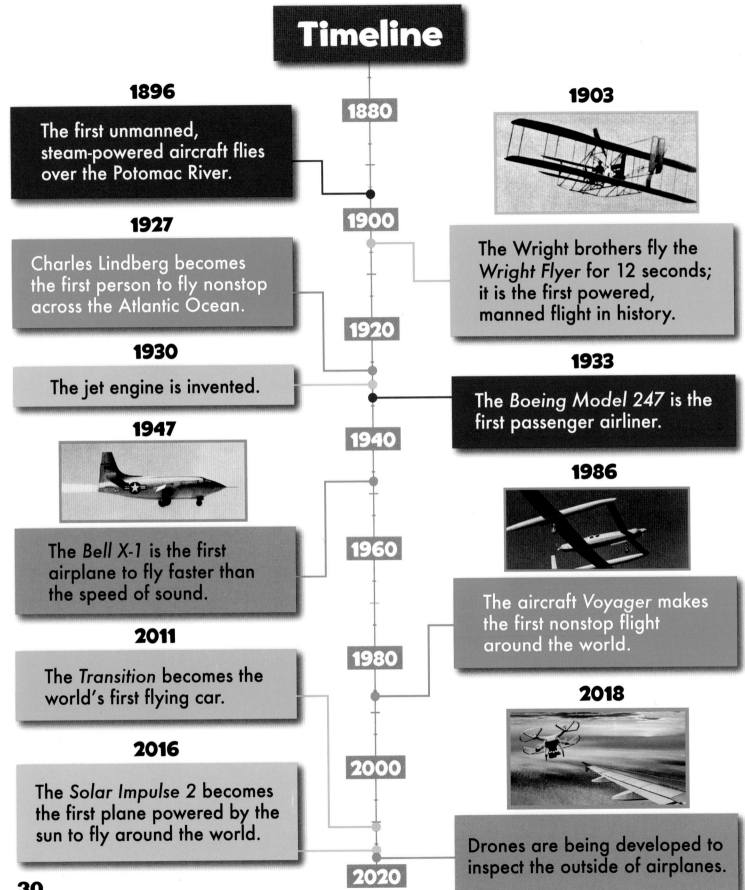

1896
The first unmanned, steam-powered aircraft flies over the Potomac River.

1903
The Wright brothers fly the *Wright Flyer* for 12 seconds; it is the first powered, manned flight in history.

1927
Charles Lindberg becomes the first person to fly nonstop across the Atlantic Ocean.

1930
The jet engine is invented.

1933
The *Boeing Model 247* is the first passenger airliner.

1947
The *Bell X-1* is the first airplane to fly faster than the speed of sound.

1986
The aircraft *Voyager* makes the first nonstop flight around the world.

2011
The *Transition* becomes the world's first flying car.

2016
The *Solar Impulse 2* becomes the first plane powered by the sun to fly around the world.

2018
Drones are being developed to inspect the outside of airplanes.

1880
1900
1920
1940
1960
1980
2000
2020

Glossary

cockpit (KOK-pit)—the area in the front of a plane where the pilot sits

descend (dee-SEND)—to move from a higher place to a lower place

design (di-ZYN)—to make a plan for how to build something

engine (EN-juhn)—a machine that makes power needed to move something

fertilizer (FUHR-tuh-ly-zuhr)—a substance used to make crops grow better

propeller (pruh-PEL-ur)—one or more blades that turn very fast; a propeller moves the plane through the air

runway (RUHN-way)—a long, flat piece of ground where a plane can take off or land

Read More

Amstutz, Lisa J. *Airplanes.* How It Works. Mendota Heights, MN: North Star Editions, 2017.

Brown, Jordan D. *How Airplanes Get from Here . . . to There!* Science of Fun Stuff. New York: Simon Spotlight, 2016.

Rustad, Martha. *Airplanes.* Smithsonian Little Explorer. North Mankato, MN: Capstone Press, 2014.

Internet Sites

Use FactHound to find Internet sites related to this book.

Visit www.facthound.com
Just type in 9781977102492 and go.

Super-cool stuff! Check out projects, games and lots more at **www.capstonekids.com**

Index

A+ Books are published by Pebble,
1710 Roe Crest Drive, North Mankato, Minnesota 56003
www.mycapstone.com

Library of Congress Cataloging-in-Publication Data
Library of Congress Cataloging-in-Publication data is available on the Library of Congress website.
ISBN: 978-1-9771-0249-2 (library binding)
ISBN: 978-1-9771-0501-1 (paperback)
ISBN: 978-1-9771-0253-9 (eBook PDF)

Editorial Credits
Michelle Parkin, editor; Rachel Tesch, designer; Heather Mauldin, media researcher; Katy LaVigne, production specialist

Photo Credits
Alamy: Dariusz Kuzminski, 30 (bottom right), INTERFOTO, 30 (top right); Getty Images: Bettmann, 30 (left and right middle), Brooke/Stringer, 16-17, Universal History Archive, 17 (inset); iStockphoto: bkindler, 10, energy, 13 (inset), frankpeters, 8, guvendemir, 20-21, Jag_cz, 12-13, muratart, 11, Rathke, 6-7, Senohrabek, 14, serts, 9; Shutterstock: CrispyPork, 4-5, Dan Thornberg, cover (top), 1, Denis Belitsky, cover (bottom middle), frank_peters, cover (bottom right), Galyna Andrushko, cover (bottom left), Gavin Baker Photography, 24-25, Igor Karasi, 15, iurii, 29, Jag_cz, 27, oriontrail, 19, PomInOz, 26, Popsuievych, 23, Sebastian stocking, 28, Skycolors, 18, vaalaa, 22, Yasar Turanli, 2-3

Printed and bound in the United States of America.
PA49